In Defense of Fraternity and Political Freedom

In Defense of Fraternity and Political Freedom

In an age of safe spaces and other abstract concepts made from nonsense I want to say I'm appalled at the current generation. It is my generation and that which I cast off.

But I came to write about the error I see in the world. I see a great liberal hypocrisy in the world I am a part of that.

Through a defense of college fraternities, an assault on the train wreck of feminism, an exposition on the absolute freedoms, and an opposition to college adjudicators I hope to expose this hypocrisy and protect the rights of the so called elite. However I assert they are not always elite.

Spaces, examples being black spaces, queer spaces, or female spaces, are in no way inclusive. They aren't meant to be. But the liberal spectrum seeks to project a narrative that spaces should be established and respected.

Unless those spaces are male spaces.

Fraternities are one of the last male safe spaces. That is one of the few remaining places for intellectual intercourse among true brothers and peers. It is inclusive of its demographic. Every fall, spring, and summer around the country young men go through the rush process and hope for bids from one of the fraternities at their college. They wish to join a brotherhood, to pledge, and to be guided through an experience that is lifelong and rewarding.

Hazing is the often uniting force that binds pledges together.

I believe hazing is permissible. I believe hazing can and does have a use and a value to the men and women who take part in it. There is a value behind what some see as an evil plague on college campuses. Others defend hazing as a necessary evil. I don't believe it is evil at all. Maybe it strengthens pledges and bonds men together. To build better men and to build brotherhood, men must face a crucible. This crucible is the hazing which builds a pledge class into men worthy of calling themselves 'brothers.' However there are examples of dangerous actions which have no value and do not strengthen men.

But politically correct universities and colleges, overrun by SJW liberals and angry geeds (read uninitiated and unaffiliated members of the university who have no wish to join Greek life or support it whatsoever) want to destroy the Greek system.

Hazing is defined as *the imposition of strenuous, often humiliating, tasks as part of a program of rigorous physical training and initiation.* Furthermore, it is also defined as *humiliating and sometimes dangerous initiation rituals, especially as imposed on college students seeking membership to a fraternity or sorority.*

In Defense of Fraternity and Political Freedom

Hazing could be thought of as wrong due to coercion. For some, being a member of something bigger than themselves, belonging to a brotherhood, and giving back are lifelong goals. Put yourself in the situation of the initiate whose parent went through what they did, and their parent before that. When you're not only answering to your pledge brothers, but to your father who wore letters before you, your grandfather who just attended the funeral of one of his fraternity brothers to conduct the funeral ritual, and your blood brother who got initiated last spring; you don't want to fail. The coercion comes naturally.

Other times the pledge coerced the older brothers to haze. A fraternity brother was asked by a pledge to brand him and the fraternity brother in turn heated a wire hanger with a torch, or lighter and branded the pledge. Still, with informed and eager consent nonetheless consequences were not far behind. In this example there is evidence that universities couldn't care less about the consent and ownership of an individual and their right to do with their body as they please.

Deception could make hazing wrong because you can't consent to something that you don't know about. However the deception is separate from the hazing. Only the deception itself is wrong. This argument is sound. But is it safe to assume that deception itself could be hazing? If I may, a personal anecdote.

Edward Masters

Often times a pledge is told they have failed. During hell week, they are left to believe they failed. But this was the final test. In this, the deception is the only hazing. It was the final test. In this test the brothers observed how the pledges reacted.

There is a necessary harm in brotherhood.

The main hinge of the necessary harm argument in support of hazing is that it builds commitment, bonding, and exclusivity. If there were other ways to build these tenets, then hazing wouldn't occur. Now by no means am I defending, for example, the merciless beating of a pledge within an inch of his life. That's assault. I am however defending, just as every other affiliated Greek should defend, hazing acts which build better men. But if hazing can build better men, then is any hazing that concludes in some form of betterment permissible? I ask myself this question because if it is true, then almost anything could be permissible given that it does not violate a pledge's consent.

Of course that consent is the blank check to do basically whatever we want. That consent is the promise the pledge made in good faith to his future brothers.

An opponent of hazing might say it is degrading to a pledge. But who are you being degraded to? The pledge is being degraded by those whom he will soon call brother. If everyone is in the same boat, and have been through this before, can anyone call it wrong? If enduring temporary subordination is simply a step toward becoming a member and joining a group, and no other violation is made, I say it's a good thing.

There is however a required clarification. The only piece of specific exemption to this philosophy is the use of Alcohol. Make no mistake, if brothers are making pledges drink copious amounts of liquor, they are putting their lives on the line. These extreme activities, unlike constructive hazing, build no brotherhood nor teach any discipline. Alcohol hazing is pointless, dangerous, and extremely stigmatized for a good reason. It can be easily substituted away with much safer activities like sleep deprivation and physical activities such as running or pushups. At least then, a passed out pledge goes nighty night and survives compared to an unconscious pledge with a BAC approaching .4 and headed on a one way trip to the morgue.

And when those un-supervised idiots die due to being left to sleep it off on the couch with a high BAC, then the entire Chapter is disbanded and those with any personal involvement wind up with criminal charges. The rest of the disbanded Chapter members gets to deal with multimillion dollar civil suits for a decade. It's an all-around lousy situation.

Pledges desperately want to impress Actives, and Pledges will enthusiastically push beyond their prior limits to do that. But in drugs and drinking, if that push beyond prior limits is not closely supervised by someone older and wiser and more experienced, then the members of the Chapter are just playing Russian

Roulette with the lives of men they want as their Brothers. Eventually the chamber will align with the round and someone will die.

'True Hazing,' if there is such a thing, is made of a crucible pledgeship that constructs a better man from the pledge that has a potential to be a better man. This is constantly reiterated because it is the simplest truth of why hazing is not bad. The crucible pledgeship, to construct and strengthen brotherhood, must involve hazing for these reasons. But this crucible pledgeship is never the product of dangerous tasks. The difference between dangerous hazing and the crucible pledgeship can be illustrated clearly by two stories at different universities.

Nolan Burch was a Kappa Sigma pledge at West Virginia University. He died after drinking. When police arrived they found him unconscious and his BAC was approaching .493. Richard Schwartz, Burch's 'big brother' was arrested in connection with the incident. While there is no way to determine whether the consumption of liquor was consensual or forced to a degree, there remains a debate. On one hand, it is possibly consensual. On the other hand, Alcohol hazing is determined to be dangerous even when it is not forced on pledges.

The 2012 Pledge Class of Delta Kappa Epsilon at The University of Alabama knew 'bows and toes' all too well. The modified abdominal exercise relies on keeping in a push up form with elbows and toes the points of pressure on the ground. In 2012, alleged use of broken glass and bottle caps in the exercise was reported anonymously to the hazing hotline maintained by UA. The university made a unilateral sweep of pledgeship, ordering all of Greek life to cease and desist any new member activities. It was criticized as an overly broad measure. DKE Rush Chair Jake Morrow defended the use of exercises as a part of crucible pledgeship, albeit in simpler terms saying, "I feel like everyone does exercises."

Hazing builds better men. By the trials and triumphs of your pledge class, you will become the great brother that will strengthen your chapter. It continues to happen because it works.

I feel as if a further defense of fraternal activities is required. This defense is of the actions and activities a fraternity engages in.

Take the case of the Alpha Tau Omega chapter which was suspended from Indiana University for a "sexual misconduct" incident originally believed to involve pledges.

The video from a smartphone showed a sex act that occurred. The event was unauthorized involving about half of the chapter's membership. The National Fraternity investigation revealed the 21-year-old man in the video was an initiated member, not a pledge, and the two women in the video were exotic dancers hired by one of the members. Their investigation revealed that no pledge was compelled to participate. Regardless, with no laws broken, a politically correct sweep of administrative vigilantism shuttered the chapter doors.

Is this a sign that hazing is such a perceived problem? Is it safe to assume that colleges and universities have become so fragile and sensitive to controversy that the slightest angering of a person in power mandates the removal of a group of good men? Maybe. It's understandable how an educational institution would want to protect itself and pass liability away from its own campus.

However there can still be a defense of hazing emphasizing its positive aspects. The elected aspects to be specific offer positive change and betterment.

Is it strange to believe that the groups which will defend actual child molesters, gang raping refugees in Europe, and twisted looters in major American cities would then vilify fraternities?

Well fraternities don't have Lena Dunham, extremist refugees, or looters from Ferguson and Baltimore.

No, Fraternities just include presidents, senators and celebrities. They just have the past, present, and future leaders.

A proven track record of great leaders is enough of a defense of fraternities. Sororities, the female equivalent, have also produced strong leaders.

Women can make good leaders. It is the strong and capable type who seek that same intellectual intercourse and comradery.

In Defense of Fraternity and Political Freedom

Sorority women have deep personal responsibility; just like fraternity men.

That deep personal responsibility is not distributed to all women.

Middle class white females, who are better off, think they have it worse than men. Now maybe this was akin to a parable of the Dunning-Kruger Effect, where those who are most skilled believe they are least skilled and vice versa, but hypocrites are everywhere. Through four years of high school and a few years of college I have listened to feminist propaganda while I am smirking at the absurdity. I ask myself, "What is feminism? Why did society need it? Do we still need it?"

Feminism; defined as either "the theory of the political, economic, and social equality of the sexes" or "organized activity on behalf of women's rights and interests" was coined in 1895. However it would take almost a quarter of a century before the first feminists secured for all women the right to vote in 1920. These first "suffragettes," as they were known, fought for fundamental legal rights not clearly enumerated before. A few decades later and building upon the foundations built by these early feminists, second-wave feminism became a household name in the mid-20th century. It stressed that women were owed the same social, political, legal, and economic rights that men have. This wave would have ended with the ratification of the Equal Rights Act, had the deadline for ratification not expired and public outcry reflected the opinion of the states, Even within second wave feminism, its vocal activists and supporters were still white, middle or upper class, and heterosexual. We call that "privilege." Because of the new found and burgeoning acceptance of homosexuality, second wave feminists began to be seen as the discriminatory faction. This, in addition to the omission of multiethnic peoples; Blacks, Hispanics and Asians in the movement, the third-wave or "Modern Feminism" begins to make gains in the late 20th century. Modern feminists stress three main issues which are to a degree interconnected. They argue that women are paid less than men, fight for total reproductive rights for women, and seek to curb domestic violence. In the same way first and second wave feminism can be seen as propagating a positive message of "all people are equal and can women can do the same jobs as men," third wave feminism emphasizes that all people, be it a cisgender white woman or a transgender black man, are equal.

This message has unfortunately been radicalized by social justice warriors. SJW's are portrayed by actual activists as being the exact problem they wish to stamp out. They are a rebirth of some of the second-wave demographics, white, upper class, but often misinformed and disillusioned to the facts of the issues they argue and the real world as a whole. Because of this, they are shunned or outright rejected from the mother cause of modern feminism. Real feminists, as they label themselves, believe that by reaching the three goals of "real" third-wave feminism, they can finally obtain liberation and equality. Feminists say our country hasn't had these two civil constructs. Facts tell a different story; but first let's see what the American public thinks.

Today, feminism as a constructive and positive force is thought dead or dying by a general consensus. 73 percent of American adults perceive feminism as a neutral or negative term. When asked if they considered themselves feminists, 73 percent of women and 93 percent of men were either sure they were not or indecisive about their standing. This was not to say they did not believe in equal rights, as only 9 percent of surveyed adults believe for some reason or another that men and women shouldn't be total equals. So what does it mean when the American public believes in equal rights but on the same hand rejects feminism? Maybe they are tired of the whole mess. They see SJW's and real modern feminists as one in the same. So maybe it's not feminism that is thought dead, it's radicalism across the board. It's the false idealism and militant hatred of a young teenage girl at her keyboard, screaming until the world listens; because she just wants to be the center of attention.

The general public says feminism is dead. They see the gynocentric activism as irrelevant. There exists the view that feminists and social justice warriors are one in the same.

At the core of their respective factions are a number of similarities.

First, we must look at an actual feminist. A feminist wants equal rights for all genders and wants equality. Because all this well thought, well spoken, and intelligent group wants is equality and rights for all; non-females are gladly welcome. Anyone can be a feminist according to most feminists. Feminists can be from any social, economic, or cultural background; as long as they want equality.

Secondly, we meet the social justice warrior. These white, upper class, but often misinformed and disillusioned "activists" are blind to the facts of the issues they argue and the real world as a whole. Usually I could talk about a person using pronouns such as him, her, them, etc. This just won't do with a social justice warrior; who identify themselves as otherkin. Some of the most outrageous pronouns are outrageous misnomers like Ze, co, hesh and thon. They are well deservedly the stereotypes of the movement; with the flawed statistics, screaming, victim complex, and such. SJW have taken something inherently good and turned it into rabid screaming matches that damage the message they are trying to spread. For instance, a white American male makes a joke. SJW's will coordinate using a bevy of websites and social networks to "dox" him. That is to publish his personal information, including where he works and lives. This is followed by pressuring the man's company by inundating it with calls and messages with the malicious goal of removing his source of income while engaging in a mass spamming campaigns to get his online accounts suspended. As a social justice warrior is more than likely rich and will never have to struggle in their life, their nebulous and hate-filled actions appear even more despicable. And for a group that is vehemently against being called "feminazis" that sounds a bit fascist. This fractional and very vocal minority are a thought police of might-makes-right rhetoric. They also seem ignorant to how the world works.

Feminists and SJW's share very few similarities. Their differences stem from how they wish to fix their respective platform issues. While feminists want to make the world better and prefer dealing with actual oppression at home, the social justice warrior is more concerned with their own country; by extension their own worldview that is clouded by their victim complex. While a feminist will attempt to fix an issue with constructive debate, a SJW will almost always have to resort to sabotage. A feminist would be more inclined to give aide to women in a third world country-a place with actual oppression- than to complain about first world problems in an echo chamber like a social justice warrior. A social justice warrior will propagate a hypocritical view that only some people are equal, while a feminist will actually strive to accomplish this goal. One large similarity, other than the whole same views differing opinions on solving issues, is the gender. Most feminists and SJW are female. They however do differ on whether they are willing to accept male help. An SJW will say "men must help and fight oppression" while simultaneously contradicting that "men can't be feminists because they benefit from oppression." In the end, it's a funny thing. Both groups are volatile and in their good meaning, but accomplish two separate missions. With the ideological, intellectual, and demographic differences, we can conclude the flaws and triumphs of both factions. So while the general public can say feminism is dead and equality achieved-a social justice warrior is going to keep typing away at her keyboard-triggered and offended. Maybe its parents should have beat it a little more.

Social Justice Warriors are afflicted with a victim complex. They bring a bad name to the fight for equality and liberation. Their three main issues; that women are paid less than men, total reproductive rights for women, and curbing domestic violence; are framed as the biggest issues in the world. This is complete and utter bologna coming from the biggest crybabies around. SJWs are the supposed masters of spin and telling half-truths. It's something that needs to be exposed and rebutted. It needs to happen soon as the cry bullies are now encroaching on expressive rights.

We value freedom of speech so much. Imagine a world where you are persecuted for what you believe in; where the slightest outspoken comment against a regime will lead to consequence by your government. We do not live in a world like this and thank our Founding Fathers for that. America is great because of the right of the people to have discourse that is not censored by our government. It is one of the simplest freedoms we have but at the same time the most vital.

In Defense of Fraternity and Political Freedom

There is a reason it is in the 1st Amendment to the Constitution. It is at least arguably, at most definitively, the most important amendment we have in this nation.

But this freedom is under attack. Not so much legally but rather culturally. There is an outspoken minority of liberal and leftist ideology which threatens this freedom. Among them are the Social Justice Warriors. But while I just stated that as of now the 1st amendment is not under attack from a legal perspective, the SJW camp would very much support censorship.

The ignorance is most common and most potent in the university administrations and on the college campuses throughout the developed world.

Colleges seem to be populated by the most liberal of liberals; complainers and cry bullies, feminazis and SJW, and lawsuit fearing administrators.

It can be observed on the university and college campuses where ignorance runs free under the guise of expression and free thought. This free thought is an excuse to attack that which has held firm in the nation for many years. The ignorance attacks the liberties of the citizenry. It is pure idiocrasy to believe that free speech should be prohibited because of how it may make someone feel. It is not hate speech to disagree with a leftist viewpoint and present your own view. It is however childish to disregard the opposing view because of some sort of trigger. Especially at institutes of higher learning.

College campuses are the last place where safe spaces like those that SJW pursue to establish should even exist.

And that's part of the point, isn't it? On a good university campus, there should be room for ALL viewpoints, for ALL cultures, and all should be allowed to express those cultures and viewpoints freely - you know, that Free Speech thing we keep hearing about.

The populace is willing to forsake our values as a nation to further their cause of political comfort and correctness. I say this is the worst idea since prohibition. Much like it, the PC culture bullies from its pulpit and seeks to restrict essential freedoms and to ruin our lives.

The right of free assembly is a paramount right we often hear about.

It saddens me deeply that colleges and universities often prohibit these rights. Whether it be requiring organized groups to release their constitutional rights or be at risk of losing them, there is no backing for these state actors to prohibit their students from assembly.

I present my examples in the case of fraternities who risked it all at The University of Alabama. They were required to, under penalty of suspension, waive their right to be searched. They would not be allowed to associate with one another if they did not abandon their enumerated rights. State actors, which the university was as a public college, cannot infringe upon these rights. Yet they tried. UA targeted Greek Life in particular.

Freedom of religion is often toted as a right. In a sense it is a right. On the other hand, the exact wording in the Constitution presents a non-connection between the state and between religions. There is a rightful separation of church and state. But the morals of being a good person cross the boundaries of religion.

Free press ties into free speech in the most basic way. It promotes that free exchange of ideas that necessitate there being freedoms so they can be expressed.

The right to keep and bear arms is an essay in and of itself. But I wish to discuss it so I shall. The argument on gun control is not one of simple truth and emotion, but of liberty and freedom.

The Second Amendment of the United States Constitution reads: *"A well regulated Militia, being necessary to the security of a free State, the right of the people to keep and bear Arms, shall not be infringed."* This wording requires an interpretation reliant on the wording of the Constitution's time. In the same landmark case of *District of Columbia v. Heller* (2008) which upheld the principle statement of the amendment were written in the majority opinion that: "its words and phrases were used in their normal and ordinary as distinguished from technical meaning." We must defer to the founders to understand the supreme law.

The privacy rights of Americans should not be infringed upon by the government. Yet at the same time, an absolute right to privacy could and does hinder law enforcement. It's almost like police need a way that they can search and seize if necessary evidence of a crime. Maybe they should also need a judge or something to sign off on a search. But what do they search? Maybe the search should only be of the places listed and it should detail what to be searched. Maybe if we had a utility to search possible criminals, we could settle on common sense privacy. Yeah. Maybe we should call it a warrant. Wait, we already have those and the government doesn't use them.

States' rights are enumerated in the 9th amendment to the U.S Constitution. All rights not afforded to the federal government are reserved to the states. It makes life easy.

Whether our rights are enumerated or God given, they are given regardless. Beyond the right of life and living, the rights of expression and defense provide an ethical and legal framework which is still used today; even in the face of those who wish to tear them away.

In another example of liberal hypocrisy and presumptiveness, there is a push for nonsensical legal standards on college campuses. Or not even legal standards. They are akin to pitchfork mobs.

In 2014, President Obama's Justice Department notified all colleges and universities that they must drastically change the way accusations of sexual assault on campus are handled. The Justice Department, under then Attorney General Holder ordered campuses to establish sexual assault tribunals under Title IX to adjudicate accusations of sexual assault - completely independent of our system of police, district attorneys, judges, juries, and courts.

As a result, right now, on every college campus in America, if a student is accused of sexual assault, the college will hold a Title IX Sexual Assault Tribunal to determine that the student is a rapist. The tribunal will be staffed by the college's Deans and Faculty – not by judges or attorneys. You cannot have a lawyer with you at your Tribunal. Neither your accuser nor the college is required to show you the evidence against you. You may not cross examine witnesses. The tribunal determines your guilt, not based on our judicial standard of Beyond a Reasonable Doubt, but rather on a much lower standard of guilt – Predominance of the Evidence. If found guilty, the college can expel you – forever.

That means that your education can be cut short by your college – forever, and all on the single unproven accusation of an angry ex.

Already, University Title IX Officers are promoting the idea that Regret is equivalent to Rape. So, if that willing and enthusiastic partner from the night before wakes up feeling not quite so enthusiastic, the college feels she is entitled to accuse you of rape and have you expelled. And you have no way to defend yourself. How, exactly, will you defend yourself when the standard of proof is The Preponderance of the Evidence? It is a he said, she said situation with neither side offering objective proof.

And right now, neither the accuser, nor the college is required to say anything about the accusations to real law enforcement – the accuser is not required to involve the police and the district attorney – who have the experience and the tools to investigate rapes and find the truth. The college's Star Chamber Tribunal operates entirely outside of the police, the courts, and the district attorney.

From the Justice Department's own statistics, from 1995-2013, only 0.2% (2 in 1,000) of college women acknowledged they had been raped (penetrated against their will) and only 0.15% (1.5 in 1,000) acknowledged an attempted rape - when asked in the National Crime Victimization Survey. When the Justice Dept added Rape plus attempted Rape plus all other Sexual Assaults plus threats of rape or sexual assault, still only 0.6% (6 in 1,000) of college women acknowledged being a victim. This isn't based on reporting to Police - and having to co-operate with Police and facing their accuser - this was an anonymous government survey - the best data the Federal Government has to date - and the same data that was used to stoke the fires that led to the Title IX Tribunals.

Sounds pretty fair I think.

If the evident sarcasm isn't sufficient, then that's a problem.

In America, we don't adjudicate serious felonies in tribunals without lawyers, judges, juries, or 200 years of settled jurisprudence, where the accused has no ability to have a lawyer present, no ability to see all the evidence in advance, no ability to cross examine witnesses, and no ability to hold the accuser's accusations to a standard under oath. We do not end anyone's future without evidence beyond a reasonable doubt. As Americans, we do not end people's future solely on he said / she said - no matter how loudly she said he did it. A couple hundred years ago, wiser men than me agreed that it was preferable to let guilty men roam free rather than punish the innocent - and so our standards for adjudicating serious felonies - like rape - are serious standards - trial by jury under oath before a judge with right to counsel and right to see all evidence and the right to cross examine all witnesses.

About the same time our Founding Fathers were enshrining our rights to due process in our Constitution, another country's leaders tried a different system, and found their different system did unspeakable damage to their history. Their skirmish with a very different system of adjudicating serious crime without serious rights began with, "J'acuse!" It did not go well. Their own leaders now refer to that dark period as, "la Terreur." We can examine how the extrajudicial adjudication of a serious felony - rape - is any different from "The Terror" that followed the French Revolution, when all it took to summon the guillotine was, "J'acuse!" and a few scattered shouts of, "Oui, Oui!" That didn't work out too well then. That's why our Founders wrote something very different.

Once, not too long ago, America too had a brief ill-advised flirtation with charging serious sexual felonies with little more than conflicting evidence. Does anyone remember the McMartin Kindergarten Rape Trials? Six years of trials without a single conviction. Why? Because the children made it all up. We declared solemnly back then that we had learned our lesson - and justice would not seek to destroy lives without real evidence.

Rape and sexual assault are not the only crimes for which colleges believe they hold supreme jurisdiction. For a range of other crimes, colleges and universities hold conduct hearings that violate at the minimum, a moral law.

No attorney present, no statement, no discovery, and no witness testimony to support the defense are often the normal circumstances of these hearings.

Many groups and lobbies wished to change the clandestine and kangaroo court aspect of college conduct boards. Two pieces of legislation would have changed that.

The Safe Campus Act (SCA) was designed to force colleges and universities to implement due process. Without a police report from the accuser, the Safe Campus Act would have barred the college from punishing the accused unless or until the accuser filed a police report. But the college was free to investigate and issue findings - findings which the college could turn over to law enforcement - real law enforcement, not tribunals headed by deans and administrators whose primary responsibility is protecting the interests of their institution. The SCA required an Accused student have the right to an attorney at the hearings.

The SCA required all parties have access to all evidence.

The SCA required the accuser to file a police Report, under oath, involving real law enforcement in the investigation, in order for the college to be able to impose any punishment on an accused student. Unless the accuser files a police report, the college cannot impose any punishment on the accused – cannot expel, cannot limit movements, cannot require an apology. By requiring the police report, the accuser puts herself at risk for criminal perjury charges and civil damages if she files a false report. Without requiring the Police report under oath, there are no consequences for an accuser who lies, kind of like "Jackie" lied at UVA, kind of like the Duke Lacrosse stripper lied, kind of like Mattress Girl lied. The list goes on and on.

The SCA did not interfere with an Accuser's ability to seek counseling and other assistance from the college. The college may provide counseling and other therapeutic services to the accuser, whether she files a police report or not. The SCA did not interfere with an accuser's ability to ask the college for protection from the accused. Whether the accuser files a police report or not, the college may help shield the accuser from the accused. The college may move the accused into another class section, away from the accused. The college may move the accuser to an undisclosed dorm.

The college may change the accuser's email, class schedule, and even the name she uses on campus. The college may even provide campus police escorts for the Accuser wherever she goes. The SCA does not interfere with an accuser's ability to ask the college for protection, and it does not interfere with the college's ability to offer protection.

The Fair Campus Act differs from the Safe Campus Act in only one way. Under the Safe Campus Act, campuses are precluded from conducting disciplinary hearings regarding allegations of sexual assault unless the complainants report the allegation to law enforcement first. The Fair Campus Act does not include that provision.

Both bills would repeal the Department of Education's Office for Civil Rights' (OCR) misguided and unlawfully imposed preponderance of the evidence mandate, returning the decision as to which standard of proof to use in these cases to individual states, campus systems, or individual campuses.

Rape is awful. Throwing an innocent man out of college and ending his future is also awful. One cannot be used to justify the other.

The right of a sexual assault accuser to have their identity protected should come with responsibility, just as all rights come with responsibility. If accusers want their identity protected, they should be willing to help protect the rest of the campus/community/town from the same perpetrator by giving statements under oath to law enforcement - so that real perpetrators can be investigated, arrested, tried, convicted, and put away.

If women want to encourage reporting of sexual assault, they should lobby for a new principle where an accuser's anonymity is shielded only if the accuser gives a report under oath and co-operates with law enforcement to find and punish the perpetrator.

No societal good flows from shielding the identity of accusers who refuse to participate in the criminal arrest, trial, conviction, and imprisonment of their rapist. In fact, societal harm occurs directly from the almost universal anonymity afforded American rape accusers without any corresponding responsibility. Because these accusers routinely shun their civic duty to co-operate with law enforcement to arrest, convict, and imprison the rapist, rapists routinely go free, free to prey on other innocents. Tying rape shield laws to a required statement to law enforcement, under oath, and co-operation throughout the difficult process, would encourage accusers to do their civic duty, and would remove more rapists from our free society. If all citizens acted as irresponsibly as rape accusers, law enforcement and the courts would grind to a halt, and crime in this country would face no deterrent and no punishment. That is in fact what has happened with rape crimes, as feminists have made refusal to co-operate with law enforcement a red badge of courage, and counterproductively made rapists fearless and unrestrained.

This whole rape culture hysteria has corroded the legitimacy of actual victims.

But if those of like mind feel that campus rape must be adjudicated outside our judicial system and in direct contradiction to student's US Constitutional Rights, then there is a truly legal way to accomplish those aims. Amend the US Constitution. But until then, the haters are punitively accountable for their abrogation of any student's rights.

May the recipe to alleviate college campuses of the ill minded and hypocritical college populations be to strengthen the lower education system?

If we wish to reform and hope to rebuild this country I truly believe that it starts with education.

The purpose of education, according to John Dewey in 1934 was "to give the young the things they need in order to develop in an orderly, sequential way into members of society." I argue that today, to be an orderly member of society, a child must learn more than his father before him. I ague also that he must learn from a younger age.

With a world that has seen the United States of America fall from a once bright glory of academia, I am appalled.

I present therefore an idea to revitalize and move forward learning in the schoolhouse. It is divided into two parts. The first plan is for children through the 7th grade. This plan is designed to create a baseline for students to then excel and gain advanced knowledge. The second plan is designed for older students beginning in the 8th grade which prescribes advanced liberal arts education by a certain grade. Topics often taught at the collegiate level are brought down to the secondary school level and taught. Broad topics are taught as to give a wide education.

The first plan is simple.

In mathematics, a full understanding of algebraic concepts by conclusion of the period is expected. Usage of these concepts to a satisfactory level is also a goal.

In English grammar, the ability to read and write effectively is advised. The ability to think critically at the most basic level is a baseline goal. The ability to question and make observations is also set. In regards to the understanding of important literary terms and figures, the student is to comprehend at least the broad strokes.

In the Sciences there are several broad goals. Each student should have a basic or intermediate understanding of how the universe functions. The history of science and the important figures in the field will be taught. The scientific method, an important tool of critical thinkers, will be utilized.

In the social sciences the history and geography of the world shall be taught; as well as the introductions to philosophy, sociology, and psychology.

For each child, in their strongest area or their pursuit, a focus shall be made to create a master of his or her craft. A focus on strengths while tutoring in weakness shall further facilitate this goal.

Be it science or medicine, a student shall be on the springboard to his or her goals. For as further outlined in the idea, the possibilities are endless through the use of a strict and stringent education which mandates accountability. Since each goal is able to be completed by the end of semester 8, the student will have options in pace which allow for knowledge to be easier to attain dependent on the mitigating factors of each student. Semester 9 and 10 exist for the student as a buffer or a rest year before university. As such, the activities prescribed are simply therapeutic as to allow for the retention of already acquired knowledge.

Due to the fact that the student can fail and try again, we simply begin teaching earlier. We waste no time. The student is held to a higher standard. Within this frame of mind and with this as reference, it seems an easier pill to swallow.

The teacher is also held to a higher standard. The goal is to remove tenure and incentives to not do a good job.

Education fell because the true emphasis on a nation's future was not implemented. No importance was placed on the future of the next generation. No child was left behind but no child was allowed to soar ahead.

The idea is born to raise the bar. If you sink you are saved but if you wade; you can stroke. You can swim until you need help. But the nation will be better. It will only become better if we allow the best and brightest to be not so few.

In Defense of Fraternity and Political Freedom

The plan for older students is much more stringent and rewarding.

In the 8th grade, the student is securely footed in his or her education with an already diverse knowledge base.

In the first semester, the student takes five courses; Algebra 1, World History, Biology, English 1, and Psychology 1. Even if the student is shaky on concepts from the previous stage of education, he or she can still flourish and catch up.

In the second semester, the student tackles Geometry, American History, Chemistry, English 2, and Philosophy.

In the third semester, the student undergoes an in-depth course on Systems of Government, Algebra 2, Human Anatomy, Modern Philosophy, and Art & Design.

In the fourth semester, the student learns Precalculus involving Trigonometry, Principles of Economics, Earth and Space Science, Debate and Rhetoric, and Theater Appreciation.

In the fifth semester, the student takes Calculus 1 and 2 involving a double block of both. The other courses taken are European Studies, Film Appreciation, and a chosen science.

In the sixth semester, the student tackles Calculus 3, African Studies, their first year of their chosen world language, and a double block of Calc based Physics.

In semester seven, Linear Algebra or Ordinary Differential Equations is taken. Also taken are courses in Asian Studies, Literature, Music studies, and a chosen science.

In the eighth semester, the final of the required mathematics courses is taken; either Linear Algebra or ODE. The second year of a foreign language is completed. English Composition, Cultural studies, and a free science are also taken.

Upon completion of the requirements, the last of which is passing either of the final two math courses, the student is awarded their certificate of completion. The final two semesters are used to finish out requirements that were not passed or resulted in a student being held back due to prerequisite issues.

Semester 9 and 10 are structured free study. Courses like Quantum Mechanics, Cultural Geography, Biochemistry, Game Theory, or teaching opportunities allow the student to further decide on their next step after completing the prescribed secondary requirements.

These course loads instantly appear as an absurdity. Who could possibly expect such talent at a young age? It is irrelevant. We must expect greatness.

The idea to create more accountability for the student is one way to better our education system. However there is also another aspect.

The value of teachers has been lost. Once, long ago, teachers were alluring. There was pride. Now, teachers are despised. We must restore the rightful respect to the profession.

By restoring accountability at all levels in the education system, we may if possible, the system shall be mended.

Education, being held to a high moral standard, and objecting stupidity, it seems, is the way to defend political freedom in the modern world.

In regards to my defense of fraternity, and of political freedom which allows for the assembly of like-minded people, there is a certain happiness. There is a feeling of goodness to belong.

Edward Masters

The Dilemma of the Trustees and the State

Within a representative republic there exists several inherent dilemmas. The collective action problem is among them. But then there also exists the problem of the trustees.

The trustee is that which is the elected official and which we then entrust to represent our interests. But to assure this, trust then must be maintained, it must be assured.

The two issues within the dilemma of the trustees are accountability and transparency.

Of accountability, and I can only speak of that which I know, I see issues within our Congress. Due in part to the reduced interest of the people to engage in the intellectual intercourse within the nation, and the predisposition to vote along the party line, useless politicians occupy seats within our House and Senate. In addition, an increased media oriented populace, create a misinformed electorate.

Furthermore, the misinformed, uninterested, and disenfranchised do not utilize their power as the electorate. If they do not vote then they do not let their voice be heard.

In Defense of Fraternity and Political Freedom

The trustees hold their responsibility to respect and apprehend further knowledge that can be communicated to their constituents. But the fact that our congressional leaders congregate and scheme in ways, such are very lazy as well, they line their own pockets through acceptable means which the American people cannot utilize. Through their exclusion from and even worse use and advantaged knowledge our Congress profits from insider trading. In addition, our congressional leaders exist as career politicians with no term limits.

Congress is not inherently broken, but rather the circumstances of our Congress twist our nation into its current state.

But our nation, the long running American experiment, can work. As such I present a plan, my proposition, to ease the issue and fix our national leadership dilemma.

Oversight through accountability and transparency form the theoretical belief behind the trustfulness and approval of trustees as I have stated before.

Term limits should be implemented within the House of Representatives. The House was envisioned as a legislative body in which a Representative could be elected and would have to answer to their constituency. In the Senate, the six-year terms were designed to allow a greater degree of freedom to the Senator to make laws. The period of the time in office also allows the Senator to not be swept out of office from some marginal period of time when a sharp rise in disapproval from the constituency develops. As such it seems only a legislative overhaul for the House is needed.

The Congress should also draw from the same health insurance they voted to make law. The Affordable Care Act created mandates and health exchanges. These marketplaces, poorly maintained and overall worse than previous privatized systems, are now being forced upon Americans. This mandate to then force Congress to use "Obamacare" seems fitting. This goes in line with Congress being held accountable to the same laws they make. So the Congress shall not be a higher class than those they represent.

In regards to the broken welfare system, our nation needs to change. First, an emphasis on the investment of people should be made. We should spend where we can predict return. Second, our nation must curtail the wasteful spending of generational welfare. By both tightening restrictions and reducing the need for government assistance, we can create a more productive nation. Third, a return to a previous argument I have made, we must mandate the betterment of education.

Due to the notion of our nation as a representative republic and of its consent to govern given by the people, the populace exists as a willful and strong power.

In Defense of Fraternity and Political Freedom

It is important to advocate for change. In some ways, a nation such as America is a willed nation of manifest destiny, the nation must be examined.

In regards to the will of powerful nations, and I assert America was once a great nation, the nation must exert this will.

In regards to the will of the populace, this is the government of the people, the nation is free. Votes and civil debate are just as, if not more, effective than war and bloodshed. The people must remember this just as the establishment does.

In regards to the will of the singular, I assert that any man whom is a lover of his country will fight for it. Thus is the will of the singular; of the patriot.

In regards to the will of the establishment, corruption is a glaring issue. The establishment seeks to maintain the status quo. That is they wish to impose their own personal beliefs not be representative of their constituents. But the establishment in our nation also belongs to the populace. They must answer to the people. They are at the will of the people if the people ever exercise their power.

It seems a radical notion to ask for anarchy but too shallow a notion to ask for continued expansive persistence of government.

The patriot believes himself to love and fight for his country. But what of the misinformed patriot? They must number a certain size and do need to be addressed. Furthermore, the populace holds the power and must include these patriots. The willed state and the trustees are integral to our nation. This willed state has several components which the people while only one of the four distinct pieces of the will statement are ultimately the building blocks of each. The trustees are elected by the people and must be refreshed of that fact.

In Defense of Fraternity and Political Freedom

References

66th Congress of the United States of America. "19th Amendment to the U.S. Constitution: Women's Right to Vote." *National Archives and Records Administration.* National Archives and Records Administration, Aug 18, 1920.

Associated Press. "'Big Brother' Arrested for Hazing in Connection with WVU Frat Death." WBOY. February 11, 2015.

Baker, Katie. "After Allegations of Hazing, University of
Alabama Cancels All Fall Pledging Activities." Jezebel. October 19, 2012.

Dewey, John. "Individual Psychology and Education," The Philosopher, 12, 1934

Gallup. *Omnibus Report.* London: Social Surveys (Gallup Poll), 2013. *Gallup Poll Ltd.* YouGov, 11 Apr. 2013. Web. 19 Jan. 2015.

Supreme Court of the United States. "Roe v. Wade." *Roe v. Wade.* Supreme Court of the United States of America, 22 Jan. 1973.

U.S. Department of Justice. "Rape and Sexual Assault Victimization Among College-Age Females, 1995–

2013." pg. 4 *www.bjs.gov.* U.S. Department of Justice, Dec. 2014.

Van Wyk, Rich. "Alpha Tau Omega Charter Revoked, IU Chapter Closed after Sex Video Surfaces." WTHR.com. October 7, 2015.